What We E

Sara Lynn & Diane James

Illustrations by Joe Wright

TWO-CAN

Our bodies need food to make them work. Food gives us energy and helps us to grow. All living things need food. Some animals, such as cows, eat only plants. Other animals, including people, eat meat as well.

Plants are living things and need food too. Unlike animals, plants make their own food, using sunlight, water and air.

Keeping the Balance

There is so much food to choose from! To keep our bodies fit and healthy, we need to eat different kinds of food. Eating too much of one kind of food and not enough of another is not good for us.

The most important foods are fruit and vegetables, grains, and the food that we get from animals.

In some countries lots of people grow their own food. They keep their own animals too. Have you ever grown anything to eat?

If you could travel around the world you would find that people in different countries have different ways of cooking and eating food. In some countries, the people eat mainly grains and vegetables. In places near the sea people may eat more fish than meat. What is your favourite food?

Food & Animals

Animals provide us with many types of food. Apart from eating meat and fish, we drink milk from cows, goats and sheep, and eat eggs laid by hens.

Milk can be turned into other useful foods. Butter, yoghurt and cheese are all made from milk. Can you think of something very, very cold that is made from milk?

Eggs are a very useful food because they can be cooked in so many different ways. You can use them to make omelettes, scrambled eggs and poached eggs. They are also used for making cakes. How do you like your eggs cooked?

6

Breakfast

If you start the day with a healthy breakfast you will have plenty of energy! Try making some delicious muesli. You can make it the day before you need it and leave it in the fridge overnight.

Get ready...
1 mug porridge oats
½ mug plain yoghurt
½ mug milk
Fruit, nuts and raisins

Get set, go!
1 Mix together the oats, yoghurt and milk. Leave the mixture in the fridge overnight.
2 The next morning, add some fruit, nuts and raisins.

Grains

Farmers grow grain crops in huge fields. Wheat is a very important grain. It gives us the flour we need to make bread. It is also used to make cakes, pasta and different types of breakfast cereals. Do you prefer brown or white bread?

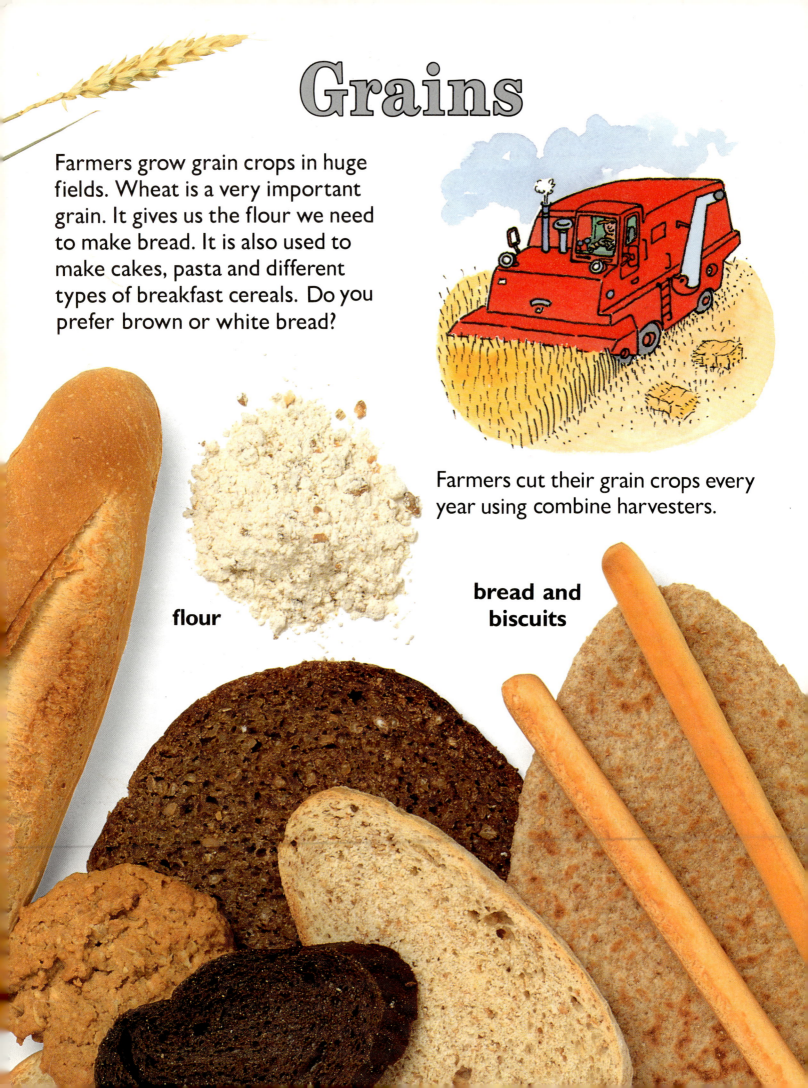

Farmers cut their grain crops every year using combine harvesters.

flour

bread and biscuits

rice

oats

barley

Rice is another important grain crop. In some countries, people eat it at every meal. Rice grows in warm places and needs lots of water. Do you like eating rice?

pasta

Animals eat grains too! Farmers often feed corn to their cows, sheep, pigs and chickens.

No-Cook Pizza

You have probably tasted a hot pizza covered in melted cheese. But did you know you can make a pizza that does not need to be cooked?
You can use lots of different types of cold food.

Get ready...
Large, round loaf
Salami, ham or fish
Tomatoes and peppers
Sliced or grated cheese
Sweetcorn and olives
Lettuce and parsley
Butter or cream cheese
Chopping board, knife and grater

Always ask a grown-up to help when you are using a knife

Get set, go!

1 Ask a grown-up to cut a large, round slice of bread from a loaf.

2 Spread the slice of bread with butter or cream cheese.

3 Start adding the sliced and grated foods. Try to make a pattern with the different shapes and colours.

Fruit & Vegetables

A fruit is the part of a plant that contains its seeds. Seeds grow into new plants. Some fruit grows on tall trees and some on low bushes.

Some fruits, such as bananas and coconuts, grow best in hot countries. They are sent by planes and boats to other countries. Which fruit do you like best?

apple

fig

dried fruit

strawberry

satsuma

banana

peppers

beans

broccoli

Strawberries grow above the ground. Potatoes and onions grow under it. Sometimes we eat the leaves of vegetables, such as lettuce, and sometimes we eat roots, such as carrots.

potato

onion

aubergine

courgette

Salad vegetables, like lettuce and spring onions can be eaten raw. Other vegetables, including potatoes, have to be cooked first.

Print It!

Get ready...
Fruit and vegetables
Paint
Coloured paper

Get set, go!
1 Ask a grown-up to cut a section from a piece of fruit or a vegetable. Look at any seeds you see inside. We used potatoes, cauliflower, apples and carrots. Try to find vegetables that have an interesting shape.

2 Use a thick brush or sponge to cover the cut surface of the vegetable or fruit with fairly thick paint.

3 Press the fruit or vegetable, paint-side down, on to a sheet of coloured paper to make a print. Try making a pattern using different shapes.

Shopping

The next time you go shopping, look at all the different ways that food is sold. Some food comes straight from farms or gardens and is sold fresh.

Some food is frozen and stored in large fridges in shops. Frozen food lasts longer than fresh food.

You can also buy food in tins. Some tinned food can be kept for a long time.

Can you find...

How many different kinds of fruit can you find in the big picture? And how many different vegetables can you spot?

Can you find the man selling fish in the market? Where do you think the fish have come from?

Can you find some of the things that you would need to make this delicious pizza?

Picture It!

Look in magazines, comics and newspapers for pictures of food. You will also find pictures on tins and packets. Pick a theme, such as our fruit, and make a picture.

Get ready...
Magazines, newspapers and comics
Labels from tins
Empty food packets
Strong paper or card
Scissors and glue

pictures cut from magazines

Get set, go!

1 Ask a grown-up to help cut out your food pictures.

2 Lay your pictures on a piece of strong paper or card. Move them around until you are happy with the way it looks.

3 Glue the pictures on to the piece of card. We painted a plate on the card first and then stuck the fruit on top.

21

Quiz

What different types of food do we get from animals?

How many things can you think of that are made from wheat?

Can you think of three different ways of cooking eggs? What is this chef doing?

Do you know what these children are eating?

Can you name these plants? Which parts of the plants can you eat?

How many of these different fruits can you name?

Index

Photo credits
p. 2-3, 8-9 © Fiona Pragoff; p. 7 Bruce Coleman;
p. 10-11, 12-13, 14-15, 16-17, 20-21, 22-23 Toby

Design
p. 16-17, 20-21 Hannah Tofts

First published in Great Britain in 1992 by
Two-Can Publishing Ltd
346 Old Street
London EC1V 9NQ
in association with Scholastic Publications Ltd

Copyright © Two-Can Publishing Ltd, 1992

Printed and bound in Hong Kong

2 4 6 8 10 9 7 5 3 1

The JUMP! logo and the word JUMP! are registered trade marks.

A catalogue record for this book is available from the British Library

Pbk ISBN: 1-85434-113-8
Hbk ISBN: 1-85434-169-3